SOUVENIRS DE VOYAGE

a traveler's keepsake book

LOUISE KOLLENBAUM

CHRONICLE BOOKS

SAN FRANCISCO

for amy and miss m

PERMISSIONS

Salon.com's Wanderlust. Copyright © 2000 by Don George from the introduction.
Reprinted by permission of Villard Books, a division of Random House, Inc., New York.

Salon.com's Wanderlust. Copyright © 2000 by Pico Iyer from the foreword. Reprinted by
permission of Villard Books, a division of Random House, Inc., New York.

The Travel Detective. Copyright © 2001 by Peter Greenberg. Reprinted by permission of
Villard Books, a division of Random House, Inc., New York.

Printed in Hong Kong

ISBN: 0-8118-3287-2

Distributed in Canada by
Raincoast Books
9050 Shaughnessy Street
Vancouver, B.C. V6P 6E5

10 9 8 7 6 5 4 3 2 1

Chronicle Books LLC
85 Second Street
San Francisco, CA 94105
www.chroniclebooks.com

Text, Design, and Illustrations: Louise Kollenbaum

ACKNOWLEDGMENTS

A heartfelt thank you to my sister, Gwen Pettus, who travels through life with me,
and to her husband, Robert Pettus, for his friendship and generosity of spirit.
To John and Charlotte Kollenbaum, who live on in memory and in their many
contributions to my art and this book.
A special thank you to Ellen and Irwin Rennert for memorable summer beach
picnics at Georgica Beach.
Anchors away to my fellow traveling spirits Candace Lyle Hogan, Diana Nyad,
Ms. Joyce Lindenbaum, Terry Ryan, Pat Holt.
To Pico Iyer, Don George, and Peter Greenberg, seasoned travelers and
consummate writers.
To editor and veteran traveler Sharon Silva, who once again set high standards.
Grazie to Francesco Paolo Viviano for the Tuscany villa of inspiration.
To traveling mentor Karon Cullen, whose many sojourns are always marked with style.
To Michael Mallery at World Litho for production, Debra Lande and Carey Jones
at Chronicle Books, and Louie Tse at DPI.
To Jim Carroll, John Boland, the inspired Stuart (Uncle Stu) Horwitz,
Charles Mize, Carla Downing, and Kathy Leonard, who contributed
their collections, travel stories, and expertise.
To Bob and Lois Meredith and Bailey for taking care of Miss M.
To Seabourn Cruises, who gave me sailing fever, for the trip of a lifetime.
A special nod to the places that inspire me: Hotel Hana Ranch, Maui; Garland's
Lodge, Sedona; The Mark, New York City; Europa e Regina, Venice; Athenaeum,
London; Chewton Glen, near Bath; Mauna Kea, Kona; Auberge
du Soleil, Napa; Bouchon, Yountville; and Ventana Lodge, Big Sur.
Finally, this book would not exist without Amy Rennert,
the ultimate companion who shares the journey.

TABLE OF CONTENTS

INTRODUCTION

My journeys are made up of many glimpses, feelings, and intuitions. And the collages that I create to commemorate these trips are layered with mementos, the small things that I loved the most.

Just as a photograph can take me back to a specific time and place, so can a pressed flower, a small seashell, or even a theater ticket stub. Reminiscences and sweet dreams are made of such things, and I travel to experience and to record and sometimes to re-create later what I have seen and felt.

A pressed grape leaf from the vine-covered patio of the Tuscan villa where Amy, my traveling companion, and I stayed brings back the entire visit: our daily walks on the winding cobblestone streets; the strains of Italian pop music mixed with the sweet sounds of children at play and the nearly constant ringing of the *duomo* bells; the local wine and *pecorino* at the neighborhood *osteria* and the celebratory dinner we ate there with two old friends. All of this is contained in that single decomposing leaf. Later, when I envision the collage, I think about combining the leaf with the wine-stained paper menu from the *osteria* and a photograph that I took of our happy group that night.

Open my heart
and you will see
Graved inside
of it "Italy"
—plaque on a
Venetian palazzo

8

A small fluorescent green eraser brings back the dramatic atrium in London's Tate Modern and the scale of the artwork on display there. I look at the eraser, purchased at the gallery shop, and my mind's eye once again sees the industrial exterior of the building, a former power plant, and the towering Louise Bourgeois sculptures housed inside it. If I stay with the day, I remember going from the Tate to the renovated Royal Theatre, where the mix of an old façade and new interior elements combined with the intermission smells of cigarettes and cocktails lingers longer than the disappointing play. The green eraser now sits on my desk, and I use it to clean up my collages.

Firecracker packaging from Garland's Lodge, a place we have returned to each year for a decade during the Fourth of July week, conjures up its own set of memories: the nightly bonfires, the rustic, nurturing cabins by the creek, and the calm that settles over us within minutes of our arrival.

A matchbook from the Rex Hotel in Saigon recalls the thick smell of the city air at dusk and the light breeze I felt as the cyclo, almost in slow motion,

carried me along the streets. At dinner that night, my companion, in trying to explain my shellfish allergy, looked too quickly at the dictionary and mistakenly told our hosts that I was selfish. They automatically averted their eyes at the embarrassment of my friend saying such a thing about me, only to have us all laughing together moments later when the misunderstanding was corrected.

10

Simple objects—a leaf, an eraser, a firecracker wrapper, a matchbook—are the triggers and touchstones that put my imagination in motion.

Now it is your turn to imagine. Carry this book with you on your next journey. Fill the blank pages with your thoughts and perhaps some simple collages made from a day's collecting, and slip other mementos into the transparent sleeves for temporary or permanent storage. Use the half-ruled pages (beginning on page 42) to record an afternoon's adventure both in words and in a sketch or collage.

I hope that my stories and images will inspire you to explore the artist in you—to create your own collages as a way of keeping cherished travel memories alive forever.

chapter one

COLLECTING
the art of collecting

Collecting comes easily to me. I am drawn to things for a variety of reasons—their shape, their color, their texture, their age, even their spirit—without worrying about how I will eventually use them. I've learned to trust that later, while sifting through my treasures, stories will unfold and my cache of souvenirs will settle naturally on a place in my compositions.

The stories sometimes describe a moment and other times an entire journey. Some are dictated by color; that is, an object finds its spot in a collage defined by a specific palette. You will discover that your stories—and your collages—will be infinite in number, told through a combination of images that layer one memory atop the other, revealing things as indescribable as emotions and as specific as a sip of single malt scotch or a pressing from a friend's garden.

When you travel, consider anything that catches your eye a souvenir, and a possible piece in a future collage: a playbill autographed by Helen Mirren, an ornate cigar band, vintage ribbons from a flea market, a colorful umbrella rescued from a mai tai, notepaper from the Europa e Regina hotel in Venice

or the Athenaeum in London. Whatever speaks to you, symbolically or visually, is collectible. The most important thing is that the object has meaning for you.

Become a photographer, too. Take lots of images, keeping in mind how you might later use them in your art. In Italy, I liked the texture of the old buildings in a medieval village I was visiting, so I shot some close-ups of the crumbling walls and used the prints as a background for a collage. Sometimes you will need to create the image you want to shoot, a challenge that may call on your powers of persuasion. In London, I asked the driver of a classic black cab to move his vehicle a few feet forward so that I could capture the Tate Modern with his old-fashioned carriage in the foreground.

Traveling is not the time to be shy. Most people are willing to share their culture and country if you express genuine interest. For example, while having a lampshade made in Venice, I asked the proprietor for some leftover fabric samples, explaining to her that they were for my upcoming book on travel collages. She was thrilled to be included. Dressed in her uniform of tiny-flower-printed cloth and a rosy pink smock, her glasses suspended from a neck chain, she began selecting pieces from around the room. By the time I left the shop, my small plastic bag was overflowing with wonderful scraps. Those fabrics will forever remind me of my afternoon with Lucy, the generous and wise woman who spoke little English but who understood everything.

Most people are happy simply to give you something. When appropriate,

offer to pay. Always be respectful and keep in mind that
individuals typically love to talk about
what they do and where they have been.

Whether I am at home or abroad,
I'm always on the lookout for a new
gem for my next composition. I have
included transparent sleeves throughout
this journal in the hope that you will be
inspired to fill them. At the end of the day, you can transfer the
overflow to clearly labeled envelopes, freeing up the sleeves for the next
outing. Just be sure to create an order for your archives from the beginning,
with dates and place names clearly accessible, and to keep to it. (More tips
on archiving appear in Chapter Five.) That way you won't waste valuable
creative time later sorting through a mountain of mementos.

chapter two

A Travel Journal

sketching your experiences in words

A travel journal is a place to begin exploring feelings and perceptions at the moment they happen—a kind of diary written when your eyes and ears are actively absorbing what is around you. Later, your words will help you recapture the emotions that will inform your collages. Writing puts me in the present and keeps me focused.

Even the most refined and polished travel journal usually begins with a hastily scrawled thought. Such immediacy is simply part of traveling, where the unexpected regularly intervenes. I always carry a small book with me, for noting ideas and recording scenes with details to guarantee later recall. "Paradise Café, Sag Harbor, watery cappuccino, warm but overcast. . . ." That handful of words is just enough to take me back to a delicious summer day spent walking around a picturesque port and looking at antiques. I had stopped for coffee and to rest and reflect, which afforded me the chance to jot down a few observations.

Rereading, later, what I had written returned me to my state of mind on

A man travels the world over in search of what he needs and returns home to find it.
—George Moore

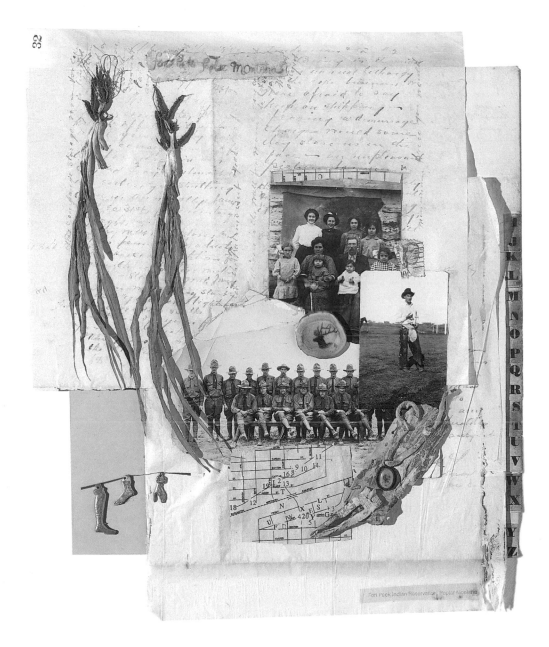

that day. I remembered feeling inspired and happy—even though the coffee wasn't good. Months later, that afternoon came alive to me again.

Writing in a journal is also a time to explore new ideas, to express them uncensored. Put aside your concerns about spelling and grammar or the desire to create that perfect sentence. You are the artist observer, sketching with words what you see and feel. Later you can choose to rewrite, but for now, like amassing the mementos for your collages, try to capture as many different scenes and experiences as possible. I heed a single simple rule: begin writing the moment inspiration strikes.

Here are some other tips to help you with your journal writing, whether you are on the road or at home:

A traveler has a right to relate and embellish his adventures as he pleases, and it is very impolite to refuse that deference and applause they deserve.
—Rudolf Erich Raspe

• Having the perfect book to read is both a pleasure and an inspiration. The art is in the selection. There are many fine travel-based memoirs, novels, and histories available. Ask other travelers and knowledgeable booksellers for ideas. Read a book about your destination before you go, to familiarize yourself with the place, then continue to read once you arrive. Discovering what others have said will spark your imagination on the road and later your memory when you begin to create a collage.

• Capture the turns of phrase and tones of voice of the people. You might hear snatches of conversation in an elevator or get ideas from articles in local newspapers or magazines. Such sources can contribute something valuable to what you already know about the place you are visiting. Just as collages are composed of "found" material, so are many journal entries.

• Shop for pens, papers, notepads, and journals while traveling. The art of writing is interpreted differently by different cultures, and new tools are always to be found. My most recent journal was written with a favorite new, bright orange Italian pen that I never would have thought to purchase at home.

• Write about a topic of special interest to you, whether it be the urban architecture, the beauty of the natural landscape, the exotic food, or a distinctive style of music or art.

I never travel without my diary. One should always have something sensational to read in the train.
—Oscar Wilde

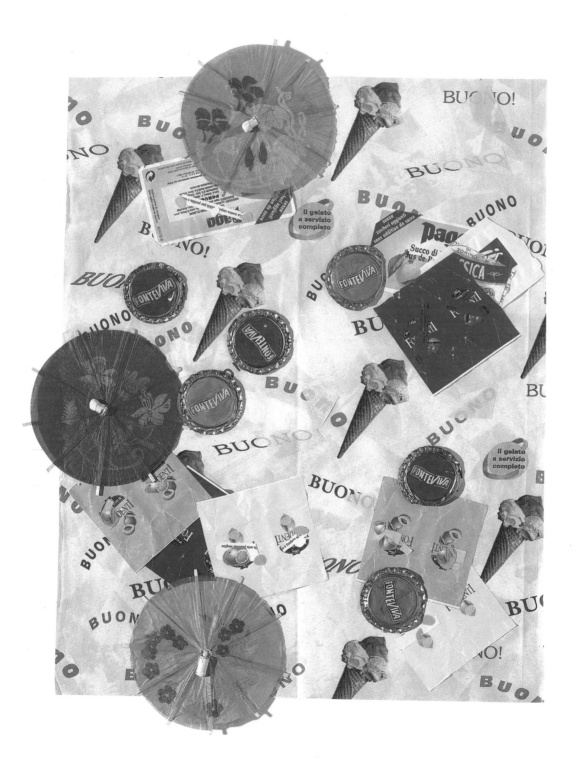

chapter three

TRAVEL COLLAGE
creating a collage from your souvenirs

Collage, from the French coller, *"to stick", is the art of arranging various materials and affixing them to a surface. The making of collages has long been part of primitive cultures, where the finished work is often believed to have magical powers. Artists active in such modern movements as Cubism, Futurism, and Dadaism also embraced this form of imagery as a means of expression. Today, the medium of collage endures.*

Establishing a space—both physically and mentally—is critical to your ability to create any artwork. Good light and large, flat surfaces are ideal. I need an uninterrupted period to let the creative process unfold, allowing not only time for work, but also time to sit and reflect. Try putting on some music. I find it helps me through the natural ups and downs of any art experience. You may even discover, as I have, that music becomes a character in what you are creating. One day while finishing a collage in which I had used a bistro place mat, wrapping paper from a charcuterie, and a Parisian matchbook, I listened to a recording of *bal musette*, traditional French café music.

For me the first great joy of traveling is simply the luxury of leaving all my beliefs and certainties at home, and seeing everything I thought I knew from a different light and crooked angle.
—Pico Iyer

21

Creating a collage is similar to working on a puzzle, with each piece informing the next until completion. However, unlike a puzzle, more than one piece can complete the collage. The first step is to lay out everything that you think you will want. Then look for something—usually just one piece—that inspires you. It might be a photograph from a trip, a ticket stub from a memorable night at the theater, or an unusual scrap of fabric or ribbon. Once you have settled on the starting point, trust in the notion that good things will flow from it.

Sometimes the memento carries a kind of charge, and complementary colors, textures, and related theme materials automatically present themselves to tell the story. While working with an antique postcard from a Paris flea market, I decided it needed a textured background. I was thinking about what might work best when I went to make lunch. As I fixed an egg salad sandwich, I realized that eggshells would create the perfect mosaic effect around the card. Imagination is my greatest tool.

As I work, I find it helpful to squint occasionally at the piece in progress. It makes it easier to see shapes and colors, and the imperfections such as glue, tape, or faint pencil marks disappear in the self-imposed blur. I also look at things up close and then from a distance. Finally, I leave unfinished pieces out and come back to them at another time for a new perspective.

Two roads diverged in a wood, and I— I took the one less traveled by, And that has made all the difference. —Robert Frost

22

Collage is a wonderfully immediate medium. It allows you to act quickly and to change and rebuild compositions easily before finalizing them. I often work on more than one piece at a time, focusing primarily on one, but continuing on others spread out in my studio. When I run out of surfaces, I put the compositions in large, new pizza boxes for temporary handling. My studio often looks like I just had a party because of the pizza box towers and because all the materials I have collected on my travels are spread out on the floor, the walls, and the shelves. It is messy, but I have a visual memory, and I like to see as much as possible at all times. Working on several collages at once is also efficient, as it allows me to select elements for more

There's always a
new corner,
a new chapter
—and who knows
what awaits there.
—Don George

23

than one composition when I go through my overflowing archives and to place my choices with their respective collages, ready for my return.

As soon as you are satisfied with the collage, the next step is to lift the various elements off the work surface so that they can be glued in place. (Adhesives are covered in detail in Chapter Five.) If your composition is simple, this will not be an issue, but if it is layered and complex, you don't want to have to depend on your memory to recall how it fits together.

If you are a beginner, perhaps the easiest way to record a construction is to take Polaroid photographs of the collage at various stages as you lift the pieces off the work surface. When you are ready to glue, use the shots to reassemble your artwork, starting from the base.

Another possibility is to use tracing paper to record the completed artwork. Once you have traced each piece of the collage, remove all the parts and use the tracing as a template to reconstruct the collage by laying it over your blank surface. Then put the pieces back in place, inserting them underneath the tracing paper. Again, start from the base and work upward, gluing each piece according to the pencil-drawn template.

chapter four

COMPOSITION AND COLOR

two fundamentals of design

Making a collage requires no formal training. You can begin creating a piece of art as soon as you have assembled the materials. Some elementary knowledge about composition and color will help produce a more successful result, however, and this brief discussion is designed to provide you with the basics and with ideas on how to apply them. Not surprisingly, volumes have been written on both topics. With luck, your curiosity will be sparked to seek out some of them.

Composition: This term refers to the placement of various materials on the page. As soon as you start to work, consider what shape you want your finished collage to have and how large it might be. I often find that my initial surface is too small, and as I build, I run out of room. Always leave yourself as much area as possible, so your work can grow and change shape as your imagination expands. Remember, too, you will need extra margin all around for framing.

Some people like to begin by sketching a composition in pencil, but I do

Cities, like cats,
will reveal
themselves
at night.
—*Rupert Brooke*

my "sketching" with the materials themselves. Pull out the images that you want as your focal point, separating them from those that will end up at the back or sides. Arrange these secondary elements around the edge of the page to help the eye flow.

If you're uncertain about what will make up the composition's central element, this is the time to experiment. Loosely arrange pieces as you go, using color as a means of getting the eye to move. For example, if red is the most vibrant color in the composition, where you place it will probably determine where the eye will go first. As you work, try to imagine how the collage—the composition—will look when complete.

Keep in mind the need for movement and for space. Diagonal lines suggest motion and energy, horizontal lines are more static, and curved ones have a softening effect. Space is important, too. Negative space is the absence of form, and art is defined as being as much about what is not there as what is there. As you shift the pieces of your collage, observe what kind of space is being created.

Color: Understanding some rudiments of color is the first step to using color creatively. Red, yellow, and blue are the traditional primary colors, but the hues that can be made from combining them are infinite. The term *value* refers to the relative lightness or darkness of a color. When a color is darker than it is in its pure form, arrived at by the addition of black, it is known as a *shade*. The term *tint* is used for a color that, through the addition of white, is lighter than it is in its pure form. Colors are also described as cool (green, blue, violet), warm (red, orange, yellow), and neutral (gray, black, white).

   All of these aspects of color give a composition form and create drama and atmosphere. Think about the mood you want your collage to evoke—is it to be somber, made up of dark browns, blues, and blacks, or festive, made up of reds, oranges, and yellows? Is it soul-searching or frivolous, playful or pensive, frantic or calm? Once you define the mood, you can begin building your palette—and your collage.

chapter five

PRESERVATION
archiving, adhesives, and preservation

Archiving

The storage of material that will go into a collage, either now or in the future, is called archiving, and its success depends on organization. After the experience of rifling through dozens of possible storage places for that one perfect piece your collage needs, you'll understand its importance, and to maintain your sanity, you'll quickly develop your own method of keeping materials. I'll share my archival system with you, but it is only one possibility. There is no correct way: the best way is the strategy that works for you.

I never want to interrupt the creative process to stop and go in search of something that I am missing. I want to have what I need on hand, or at least something similar that I can use as a placeholder until I find the ideal piece. Because of this, I have an abundance of materials available to me as I work.

Not all artists agree with this philosophy. I once overheard a teacher advising her students to limit the volume of material they collected, so that they would not be overwhelmed by it when they set to work. My approach is

ade Maraîchère
ed greens, Dijon mustard vinaigrette
$7.50

Moules au Verjus Roug
mussels steamed in red verjus, leeks, garlic & thyme
served with french fries
$15.95

A L

Pommes Frite
french fries
$3.50

Betteraves, Endives et Noix
et & endive salad, toasted walnuts,
sh goat cheese & walnut vinaigrette
$7.75

Gnocchi Saisoniers
sautéed gnocchi with a summer vegetable ragoût
$14.95

Laitue
ibb lettuce with garden herbs
$6.50

Tartine du Jour
open faced sandwich served with french fries

Chou-fleur
cauliflower gra
$3.95

Poireaux Frais
chilled leeks vinaigrette
with egg mimosa
$7.50

Purée de Pon
de Terre
potato pur
$3.50

Pâté de Campagne
ntry style pâté with watercress,
cornichons & radishes
$8.50

FROM

DESSERTS

(Served with ho

Crème Caramel
caramel custard
$5.50

Fr

Rouhe Baron
cows milk

Hu   n V lley   pert
sheep & cows milk

Pot de Crème
infused custard
$6.50

Redwood Hills Crottin
goats milk

cows milk

Crème Glacée/
Sorbet de Fruits
ice cream/sorbet
$1.50/scoop

$7.75 ea. / 3 pc (tasting portion) $9.75

maître d'hôtel butter &

Steak Frites
a pan seared flatiron served with

$18.50

Foie G

Grand Plateau
l lobster, 16 oysters, 8 shrimp,
lams, 9 mussels, seasonal crab,

RUIS DE ME

exactly the opposite. I like to have lots of material visually accessible—more than I need for a particular composition. Because I often work on more than one piece at a time, looking around at the walls, the tabletops, the shelves, and the floors in my studio gives me ideas for the composition at hand as well as others in progress.

Any surface is fair game for my archives. I display materials not only horizontally, on shelves, tables, and counters, but also vertically, attaching them to large foamcore boards that I prop against my studio walls. I tape and pin items to the boards, sometimes in groupings, sometimes alone. For example, one wall of my studio is organized by theme. When I return from traveling, I put items together that I collected on a particular outing. I find keeping things this way helps to identify the time frame of the journey and allows me to find a remembered piece quickly.

If an item does not rely on a specific event for its meaning, I might keep track of it by its palette. I like to put harmonious colors together and then play around with various combinations on whatever surface I am using. I also gather materials of the same type in one place. For example, I have one folder for antique paper with text, another folder for envelopes that bear stamps, a box for ribbons, another box for fabric, and yet another for small three-dimensional items.

As I have previously noted, I archive my unfinished collages in unused pizza delivery boxes, as they are both inexpensive and stack flat. I label the box sides with a broad-tipped marker to refresh my memory about what is inside.

Adhesives

There are many adhesives on the market today. I have listed the major ones here, but it is always best to experiment. Find an item similar to the one you want to use in your collage, or a piece of the item that you won't be using, and try adhering it to the material on which the collage will be assembled. Mixed-media collages require either a versatile adhesive or the use of different types. Never use adhesives without proper ventilation.

Spray adhesives are effective for attaching paper to a variety of surfaces. They dry quickly, appear clear, and have a matte finish. I find them effective but often messy to use. A word of caution: many sprays make it difficult to pick up something and reposition it once it has been put in place. Review the information on the container before purchase.

Rubber cement produces an effective bond between paper and many types of materials, including hard surfaces. It dries quickly without wrinkling or curling. But it can discolor paper and loosen over time, and for that reason I seldom use it.

Glue sticks, usually of paste and sometimes of liquid, are effective adhesives for bonding papers. I find the stick shape clumsy to manipulate but easy to carry when I travel.

YES Glue is a favorite paste glue of mine that works well with paper, especially thin papers. It does not cause wrinkling or shrinkage and can be diluted with water if it is too thick. It is not acid-free, however, and this affects preservation (see below). I apply the paste with my finger and have found the tactile quality satisfying. If any glue is left on the page, it has a slight gloss in certain lights when it dries. You can, however, remove the extra glue with water before it dries. I use this adhesive for most of my collages.

White glues are common, often inexpensive, and can be diluted with water. Some can even be washed away completely after they have dried.

Preservation

To preserve and store collages is a challenge. They are often comprised of many different types of material and most effective preservation is specific to a single material. The following guidelines will help you preserve not only the final collage, but also the various elements that make up the artwork, including photographs, textiles, and paper.

Paper is often the predominant collage element. Unfortunately, it is vulnerable. Most papers produced from the nineteenth century until today, including the papers and sleeves in this journal, have been made with acid, which causes the breakdown of cellulose fibers. For long-term preservation, mount your collages on acid-free paper or board, selecting a paper or board weight that will not bend under normal pressure. If you choose to mat and frame your images, again use only acid-free products.

Storage containers such as boxes or folders also should be acid-free. Boxes with reinforced corners will prevent damage; snug covers will keep out dirt. Try to store boxes flat in a dry area with a stable temperature.

Select containers larger than the original image to avoid crimped edges. Do not use newsprint when handling artworks, as it has a high acid content and may stain the adjacent paper. Self-sealing plastic bags may cause paper made with acid to deteriorate more rapidly.

Finally, do not use ballpoint or felt-tip pens for labeling collages. The ink may bleed through the top layer and damage the work.

chapter six

ENLIGHTENED JOURNEYS
traveling with an eye to preserve

Travelers are adventurers. The act of leaving what is familiar for what is unknown alters how you see the world and illuminates your horizons. I love the process of researching a trip before I set out, as it encourages a wonderful sense of anticipation and endless dreaming. I buy big maps and thick guidebooks and study them intently.

Once on the road, I travel to experience the place, to record my thoughts about it, and, sometimes, to re-create later what I have seen and felt. This journal does double duty: it is an excellent place to begin storing artifacts from any journey and it is a helpful organizing tool. Don't wait to begin sorting your treasures. Label the journal sleeves and, as you fill them, write and perhaps sketch on the pages next to them.

Just as the writer in you wants to record the moment in words, the artist in you wants to record it in images. Some of the best travel journals I have seen have combined text and artwork, both done on the road, so use the blank journal pages for creating some simple collages, too.

If you are traveling and the sleeves are suddenly full, or if you are using the journal to collect by day and then transferring your material out of the sleeves at night, consider what types of storage options are available locally. When Venetian merchants close their shops for the day, the streets over-flow with blankets filled with knockoffs. I fell in love with an imitation Louis Vuitton bag, in childhood pink with a 1950's gloss, which became a keepsake and a place for storage. The Italians are also makers of fine papers, so I bought various folders and envelopes to house what I had collected.

On a long journey even a straw weighs heavy. —Spanish proverb

Music is a source of inspiration to me when I make collages. My friends Mark and Marilee know this, and they suggested I do what they do when they travel: take a small tape recorder to catch the music, voices, and other sounds of the streets. Even the very act of bringing a recorder along reminds you to focus more on the present, just as carrying a journal does.

I found this out when I took my tape recorder for a "dry run" in my hometown of San Francisco. As I walked toward the harbor, with the city's famous fog rolling in, I recorded "Amazing Grace" played by the chimes in the Ferry Building tower, but I *heard* the chimes, too. On Market Street, I captured the sounds of an elderly man playing a sorrowful melody on a violin. Dressed in wrinkled coat and tie, he drew his bow across the strings proudly and with precision, and his face showed the passion of the music—a passion I still remember every time I listen to that "found" recording.

Books, like a tape recorder and a journal, can help you enter more fully into the life of your destination. They can be heavy, however, so it is a wonderful treat to send them to your arrival point ahead of time. Try to read subject matter close to the heart of where you are. While ensconced in a Tuscan hill town one summer, my traveling companion and I began reading *Under the Tuscan Sun* by Frances Mayes. Reading out loud to each other became a restful afternoon ritual: the old villa where we were staying was in the process of being restored, just as the house in the book was, and as my eyes wandered over the distressed yellow plaster walls, I wondered what they would look like when I returned the next year.

A remarkable thing happened when we left the country-side for Florence. I no longer had an interest in reading that particular book. My imagination had moved on, and my reading had too.

Clearly, reading is a terrific way to prepare for a trip, but so is conversation. While calling to rent a car for a

visit to Montana, I found myself on the phone with an agent in Bozeman. As is the custom in those parts, he acted as if he had all the time in the world to help me. It turned out that he regularly drove the route I was considering, and he told me in detail about the terrain from the city of Billings to the small town of Poplar, on the Fort Peck Indian Reservation. The more he talked, the more enthusiastic he became, and the more excited I got about driving instead of flying. He described the Badlands vividly, and I could see the rolling hills, rugged and full of gullies. I even learned what a gully washer is—a rain so hard and so long that it washes everything away—and I was immediately hooked on the road trip. It was an inspiring call, one that grew out of the everyday act of renting a car.

I am an inveterate collector, of books, of music, of conversations, and I try to convert others to my ways, to engage my traveling companions or even friends traveling elsewhere in this rewarding process. Sometimes people who initially have no interest in collecting find that looking for treasures makes them more aware of their new surroundings. When my friend Jim returned from Beijing, he was packing a folder full of newspaper headlines, postage stamps, spent tickets, and other paper memories. He said he had never before paid this kind of attention to graphics and it excited him. An outsized receipt for two martinis resembled an official document, and it was unlike any bar check I had ever seen. His carefully gathered mementos, like photographs, led to tales of his trip.

One of the best tips for ensuring an enlightened journey is to go where

the locals go. For example, getting your shoes shined in America— whether you are a man or a woman—can be fun and rewarding. Sitting in the chair and watching your dusty shoes regain their shine is an excellent way to hear local history and colorful stories. I find that most people are proud of where they live and that they love to talk about the place they call home.